Increase Your
Mind Power

Increase Your Mind Power

Improve your mental fitness and maximize your potential

JIM REES

**LONDON, NEW YORK,
MUNICH, MELBOURNE, and DELHI**

Produced for Dorling Kindersley
by **terry jeavons&company**

Project Editor	Fiona Biggs
Project Art Editor	Terry Jeavons
Designer	J. C. Lanaway
Special Photography	Mike Hemsley
Senior Editor	Simon Tuite
Editor	Tom Broder
US Editor	Margaret Parrish
Senior Art Editor	Sara Robin
DTP Designer	Traci Salter
Production Controller	Stuart Masheter
Executive Managing Editor	Adèle Hayward
Managing Art Editor	Nick Harris
Art Director	Peter Luff
Publisher	Stephanie Jackson

First American Edition, 2007

Published in the United States by DK Publishing,
375 Hudson Street, New York, New York 10014

07 08 09 10 11 10 9 8 7 6 5 4 3 2 1

ED254—September 2007

Copyright © 2007 Dorling Kindersley Limited
Text copyright © 2007 Jim Rees

Published in the United Kingdom by Dorling
Kindersley Ltd.

A catalog record for this book is available from
the Library of Congress

ISBN: 978-0-7566-3171-0

DK books are available at special discounts when
purchased in bulk for sales promotions, premiums,
fund-raising, or educational use. For details, contact:
DK Publishing Special Markets, 375 Hudson
Street, New York, New York 10014 or
SpecialSales@dk.com.

Printed and bound in China by Leo Paper Group
Discover more at www.dk.com

Contents

1 Know Your Mind

14 How Your Mind Works

18 Understand Your Behavior

22 Program Your Mind

24 Be Like a Child

2 ABC of Success

30 Be Aware

36 Challenge Your Beliefs

38 Change Your Beliefs

42 Commit to See It Through

50 Identify the Causes of
Failure

3 Stay in Control

56 Choose Your Attitude

60 Don't Play the Blame
Game

64 Slow Down and Take Stock

68 Perform Well Under
Pressure

72 Act As If It Were Possible

4 Exercise Your Mind

80 Increase Your Memory

84 Be Creative

88 Communicate Better

92 Use the Power of
Visualization

5 Mind Over Matter

100 The Power of Words

102 Know What You Want

106 Coach Yourself

112 Interact with Others

118 Index

120 Acknowledgments

Introduction

Is it possible for people to live their whole lives asleep? Or to be running so fast on the treadmill of life that they haven't had time to unravel who they really are and what they really want. Do either of these sound like you?

Increase Your Mind Power explores how your mind works and helps you to understand where your beliefs and behavior have come from. With an increased awareness of your unique thinking and learning styles you can use the exercises within this book to expand your mind power, to stay in control when you are under pressure, and to access your mind power whenever you need to.

> **You'll find success when you know how to look for it**

You will be able to apply the new tools immediately and integrate them into your work or personal life, so that you can tap into your potential more consistently. You'll notice that things that once caused you to lose control no longer have power over you. You will be able to control your mind, instead of your mind controlling you.

The ABC of Success in chapter 2 can be used in any situation to help you gain clarity through awareness, check and challenge your beliefs about what is possible, and maintain your commitment to seeing things through to completion.

By taking a mixture of universal laws and putting them into a melting pot with Eastern and Western philosophies, this book provides a guide and a shortcut to success in your life. You will find some of the strategies for success used by great leaders and thinkers of the past and the present, distilled into an easy-to-use format to help you to realize your potential.

Ultimately, the book's goal is to wake you up to the idea that we all have greatness within us. It will help you to do more, be more, and have more in your life, both personally and professionally. Whether you want to get in shape, lose weight, give up smoking, be promoted, increase your ability to concentrate, learn to respond in a more positive way to life's curve balls, or know how to coach yourself, these simple-to-follow and easy-to-apply formulas and strategies will give you the framework within which to achieve your goals.

Assessing Your Skills

These questions have been designed to assess the way you use your mind power. To gain the full benefit, complete the questionnaire twice—once before you read the book and again after you have read it and done all of the practical exercises. The more honest you are with yourself, the greater the benefits you will enjoy.

Before **After**

1 When things go wrong, how quickly do you pick yourself up and bounce back?

A I expect things to go wrong and I am weighed down by these experiences.
B It usually knocks me down and takes me at least a day to recover and let it go.
C I pick myself up quickly and see what lesson I can learn from the experience.

2 How much personal responsibility do you take for everything in your life right now?

A I believe that I don't really have very much control over the quality of my relationships, weight, health, and general well-being.
B I believe that life is a lottery and some people are just born lucky and I deal with it the best I can.
C I believe that life is what you make of it and I take full responsibility for everything.

3 What image do you have of yourself?

A I am usually clumsy and awkward and get things wrong by not being sufficiently careful.
B I'm an average sort of person and I don't think I'm any better or worse than others.
C I am unique and have a great deal to offer.

4 How do you respond to meeting new people either at work or socially?

A I am very quick to judge them.
B I am initially open and will judge them once I have gotten to know them a little better.
C I accept that we are all different and value other people's perspectives and opinions.

5 Do you set yourself goals in your life?

A I have no clearly defined goals and just let life happen to me.
B I know roughly what I want but I haven't planned it out to the last detail.
C I have clear goals for all aspects of my life.

6 How do you respond to change?

A I don't like change and usually stick to what I know.
B I struggle to adapt to change and just do my best.
C I know that change is a constant and I am flexible and will try different ways of doing things.

7 How good is your self-awareness?

A I'm not really aware or in touch with my body or how I feel and I rarely follow my intuition.
B I sometimes pick up on stress within my body and am occasionally aware of how I am feeling and the impact this has on me.
C I listen to my body and am in touch with my feelings and keep them under control.

8 When interacting with other people, how good are you at picking up on how others are feeling?

A I am not very good at reading other people or picking up on how they might be feeling.
B I am no better or worse than others at sensing these subtle changes in people.
C I am very aware and sensitive to other people's feelings and notice any changes.

	Before	After

9 **What do you do when the going gets tough?**

A I usually lose interest and lower my goal.
B I get caught up in why it won't work and find it hard to focus, but usually get there in the end.
C I focus on what's working and don't give up until I get it finished completely.

10 **At what pace are you running your life?**

A I very rarely have time for myself, have lost touch with friends, and spend less time with my family.
B I manage to keep in touch with some friends and any spare time is taken up with my family.
C I ensure that I plan time out for myself as well as having a good balance with my friends and family.

11 **Are you good at delegating to others?**

A I tend to do most things myself because I know I can rely on myself and my ability to get things done.
B I will delegate to people who have proved that they can get the job done to my high expectations.
C I believe that as long as I give clear guidance to any of my colleagues, I can trust them to do a great job.

12 **How do you react under pressure?**

A I find that I have little control over my feelings and how I express myself.
B I keep a firm control of my feelings and find it difficult to express myself.
C I am completely in control of my feelings and I express myself appropriately.

Final Scores

	A	B	C
Before			
After			

Analysis

Mostly As

These answers suggest that you have little control over the events in your life. You are not very outgoing and find it difficult to pick up on other people's feelings. One of the quickest ways to enrich your life is to slow down and celebrate all of the good stuff. If you want to change, follow the steps in the book and do the exercises (don't just read them).

Mostly Bs

You expect things to go wrong but you hope that they will turn out well, and this means that you are sometimes pleasantly surprised. You have some awareness about yourself and others. Your planning lets you down and you could be achieving so much more in all aspects of your life.

Mostly Cs

You are highly self-motivated and are in touch with yourself and others. You take full responsibility for the things you can control and are well organized. Just make sure that you don't take on too much and forget what is important to you. There's no harm in taking a closer look at your goals to ensure you are still on track.

Conclusion

If this is the first time you have done this self-assessment, then bear in mind this analysis as you read the book. Pay special attention to the areas highlighted by your responses, as well as the tips and techniques—these will help you to reduce the number of A responses next time around and achieve a more balanced mixture of Bs and Cs. After you have completed the book and put the techniques into practice, retake the assessment. Giving honest answers will enable you to get a direct measure of your progress in dealing with the areas requiring improvement—and you will see a big improvement as long as you apply these techniques consistently. Remember that any change can happen in a heartbeat and that it will be created twice, first in your mind then in reality. The change you are looking for will be a direct result of what you focus your thinking on, sometimes 3–6 months before the physical change occurs. To get in shape, for example, it will have been the thinking and training you did 3–6 months ago, not what you thought and did yesterday.

Know
Your Mind

1

By understanding how your mind works and how you store and access information you can start to maximize your mind power. We all have the ability to develop our brains to enable us to do more, have more, and be more. In this chapter you will learn:

- How your mind works and how to access information effortlessly
- To understand your behavior and conditioning and how to let go of the past
- How to program your mind and understand the left and right brain
- How to recognize the child within and distinguish between childlike and childish behavior

How Your Mind Works

Your mind is like an air traffic controller, taking in information and directing it according to its current knowledge. New information is stored as it comes in— each time you access it, the more hard-wired it becomes.

Access Your Information Highway

Access to hard-wired information becomes increasingly easy because of that neural pathway's high usage. When you start linking thoughts together and making connections, your mind lays down a neural network. This is like a busy highway with smaller dirt roads running alongside it. The highway carries the information held in the more frequently accessed parts of the brain, and the dirt roads carry information that is rarely accessed.

What Your Mind Does

Mind and body constantly interact. Your mind regulates your breathing pattern, but you are not consciously thinking about it with every breath. It ensures that your heart doesn't skip a beat, but if it does, it will come up with an explanation of why. The mind's capacity is

Your Superhighway Hard-wiring postive thoughts can become a habit. The more cars/positive thoughts you have, the easier it becomes to access.